The No Cry Sleep Solution

The Complete Sleep Solution Guide for Babies and Toddlers by using only Gentle Methods!

Get Your Little One to Sleep through the Night Now by using these Effective Yet Gentle Methods

Table Of Contents:

Introduction

I want to thank you and congratulate you for downloading the book, *"The No Cry Sleep Solution"*.

For parents, raising a baby is a very rewarding experience. Nothing compares seeing your baby smile at you, or listen to him say, "Mommy". Ah, the joys of parenthood. Although having a baby brings you joy, it is also a very daunting experience. Some parents struggle putting their baby or child to sleep. If you are one of those few parents who keep losing sleep because of their babies unpredictable sleeping patterns, don't worry. This book is written especially for you. The solution to you problem is within this book. Yes, there are gentle and effective ways to put your baby to sleep every single night. After reading and applying the tips provided in this book, you can now say goodbye to sleepless nights.

This book contains proven steps and strategies on how to get your little ones to sleep soundly through the night. The book also includes why your baby or toddler cries, how to soothe a crying baby or toddler, and helpful tips on effective parenting. The tips included in this book are tried and tested formulas. Parents who applied these solutions have now significantly improved the quality of their sleep. Read on to find out how you can benefit from this book.

Thanks again for downloading this book, I hope you enjoy it!

reparation, damages, or monetary loss due to the information herein, either directly or indirectly.

Respective authors own all copyrights not held by the publisher.

The information herein is offered for informational purposes solely, and is universal as so. The presentation of the information is without contract or any type of guarantee assurance.

The trademarks that are used are without any consent, and the publication of the trademark is without permission or backing by the trademark owner. All trademarks and brands within this book are for clarifying purposes only and are the owned by the owners themselves, not affiliated with this document.

Chapter 1: Sleep Facts

For babies

Have you ever heard of the phrase, "sleeping like a baby?" This phrase, associated with a long and deep sleep, doesn't apply to real babies. In reality, babies sleeping time is anything but long. Although they sleep for about 16-19 hours a day, they often wake up after only a couple of hours and goes back to sleep. And since they still cannot differentiate night from day, they often wake up at ungodly hours, when you're already in deep slumber. When this happens, your sleep is disturbed. You get restless in the morning and are easily stressed out. If you have been caring for a new-born baby, you would know how exhausting it is to care for an infant. To help you cope, it is important for you to understand, especially if you are a first-time mom, how babies sleep.

- It takes 20 minutes for a baby to enter into a deep sleep. Mothers need to understand that babies don't sleep right away. If carrying your baby is your way of putting her to sleep, notice your baby's breathing first. If it is irregular and she tries to smile while sleeping, she isn't in deep sleep yet. Do not put her on the bed if you don't want to keep repeating the process. Your baby is more likely to wake up if she is in light sleep. Wait until her breathing becomes regular and she completely relaxes before you put her down on the bed.

- Babies often wake up at night. Getting uninterrupted sleep for mothers during the night is almost impossible, but parents need to understand that it is for her baby's benefit. Since a baby's tummy is still tiny, she needs to be fed every few hours to fulfill her basic needs. Switch places with your spouse every other day so both of you can at least get a good night's sleep every few week nights.

- Babies sleep a lot. The only inconvenience about this fact is babies sleep for only a few hours and stay awake for a couple of hours. Then goes back to sleep. If you're not used to this sleeping pattern, things will be very difficult for you. Don't worry though as this is only temporary. Eventually babies tend to adapt to your sleeping pattern over time.

- Every baby is different. You may notice that other babies are asleep during the night while yours stay wide-awake. This is normal. Parents need to understand that no two babies are alike. As your baby grows, she will find it easier to sleep.

For toddlers

As your child grows, he or she becomes more imaginative. It will be normal for your toddler to be afraid sleeping alone.

Sometimes they tend to imagine things that interrupt their sleep. When this happens, just assure your child you are always there for him.

- Toddlers need only about one or two naps a day. Some kids do not take naps in the morning. They play and take their naps in the afternoon.

- Toddlers need about 10-14 hours of sleep every day.

- Some kids need a stuffed animal or a blanket to sleep. Parents need to make sure toys aren't dusty to prevent allergies and other sickness.

- Most toddlers do not want to fall asleep. They are very active. They want to be outside always. Allow your child to play during the day

and remind him to go to bed early at
night.

- Toddlers tend to be very talkative
  before bedtime. Sometimes they just
  won't stop talking.

Knowing these sleep facts would help you
understand your baby and toddler more.
As you spend time with your kids, you'll
notice some of their sleeping patterns and
begin to adapt to it.

Chapter 2: Why is your baby crying?

Babies are adorable little creatures. They are stress-relievers. When you're exhausted from work and you see your baby smile, it takes away all your fatigue. What a baby does is bring colors to your world. Suddenly, life has meaning. She is your reason for living. Although it can be blissful raising a baby, it is tedious to put them to sleep. Many parents struggle with it. If you have a baby who cries a lot and finds it extremely hard to fall asleep, you may want to find out why. You would be able to resolve the problem once you understand why your baby is crying. This list will help you find out the reason why your baby cries.

- Your baby may be hungry. Hunger is almost always the culprit why a baby cries. That's how she communicates that she wants to be fed. Try to remember the last time you fed her milk and if it's about time to feed her again. Watch out for other signs like a baby sucking her finger. That's a sure sign your baby is hungry.

- Your baby wants to sleep. Another reason why babies cry is simply because they want to sleep and they aren't comfortable with their position. Some babies sleep when their mothers carry them. Some sleep with a background music on. It is different for every baby. Once you figure this out, your life becomes easier.

- Your baby doesn't want a dirty diaper. Perhaps she has been wearing it for hours and it needs to be changed. Or your baby may have pooped on her diaper. Sometimes the only solution is to change. Once you do, your baby will usually stop crying.

- Your baby wants you to carry her. Perhaps the reason your baby is crying is she wants you to hold her. Babies are very attached to their mothers. They can even recognize their scent. If after you hold her she stops crying, try to cuddle her or put her to sleep.

- Your baby may be sick. If your baby cries for hours and doesn't stop, especially after feeding her, you may want to see a doctor. Perhaps she is having problems with her tummy.

- Teething. If your baby is between 4-7 months old, you may want to check her gums. At this age, babies usually get teeth already and it's painful.

- Your baby just feels like crying. This is very normal. There are babies who cry for no reason at all. If your baby cries persistently for at least three hours, she may have colic. This crying condition is normal for a healthy baby. This usually occurs when your baby is about 2 weeks old, but it goes away after four months.

How to find out what he's crying about

For a first-time mom, it might be a little difficult to find out why your baby is crying. As you spend more time with your little one, you tend to recognize patterns and certain behaviors that allow you to determine the reason why your baby is crying. You could also check this list.

- You may have noticed that newborns have a very high-pitched voice. This doesn't always mean that your baby is in pain. That's just how babies cry.

- You will notice a baby is hungry when he fusses and squirms. When this happens, feed your baby right away.

- If your baby is in pain, you will have a hard time consoling him. You will also see it in your baby's face that he's in pain.

How to Soothe a Crying baby

Consoling a crying baby is one of the most challenging jobs of a parent, but we are offering some of the gentle ways to soothe your crying baby. The first thing you should do when your baby starts crying is take a long deep breath and go with the basics. Feed your baby and change her diapers. Sometimes this will do the trick. If this doesn't work, just stay calm and try these tips:

Rock-a bye baby. Gently hold your baby in your arms and swivel back and forth. This often works, but try not to overdo it. When you keep doing this every single time your baby cries, she becomes dependent.

- Go with a soothing sound. Sometimes noises make a baby cry. Experiment with different background music and see which will work for your baby. You may want to sing to her as well. Sometimes she responds more to that.

- Get your baby outside. They like looking at things especially colorful things. A change of scenery may calm and stop her from crying.

- Get a swing for your baby. Movements help calm the baby. Create one specifically designed for your infant or toddler. Again, don't overdo this else your baby becomes dependent on the swing. She might not be able to fall asleep without it.

- Try the 5 S's. The 5S are Swinging, Swaddling, Sucking, Side soothing, and using Sshhing sounds. Wrap your baby in a blanket or hold him on his side. You may also want to give your baby a pacifier.

- Give your baby a soothing massage.

- Check if the temperature inside your house is either too warm or too cold for the baby.

- You may also want to check your baby's clothes. Perhaps they are too tight and she needs to change it. Always use loose clothes for your baby. They sleep better with those.

- Talk to her gently. A baby listens to the mother. One of the most effective ways to soothe a baby is to talk to her quietly. Assure her that you will always be there for her.

- Distract your baby with a toy.

- Carry your baby. That makes her feel safe and secure.

- Sometimes bathing can do wonders for the baby. Try giving your baby a warm bath before bedtime.

Try all the strategies mentioned above and see which one works for your baby and keep doing it.

How to Soothe a Crying Toddler

Do not tolerate negative behavior. It is best to start disciplining your child early. If your baby demands something you cannot give and he starts to cry, do not give in. Try not to let your anger set in as well. Be gentle with your child and refuse.

Give him something to do. A toddler likes to play during the day. Take him to a playgroup or any trips where there are other kids. This will surely make him tear-free.

There are times when you need to give in. If your toddler wants something, reconsider. Do not say no right away. If it doesn't harm him or your budget, say yes. That will surely stop his tears.

Chapter 3: Gentle Ways to Put your Baby to Sleep

You may have tried all the ways of putting your baby to sleep, and they don't seem to work. Every day, you keep losing sleep because your baby is awake when it's time for you to sleep. If you are a first time mom, you may want to recognize sleeping signs from your baby first so you would know if he is ready to sleep or not. You need to spot signs if your baby is already tired. Look for these signs from your baby:

- The baby rubs his eyes and tries to cry

- The baby suddenly loses in interest in whatever he's doing. When he's playing with his toys, he throws it away

- If you're carrying him, he may suddenly bury his face in your chest.
- The baby suddenly becomes quiet

These signs are telling you that it's time to put the baby to sleep. Put him down on his cot and let him take his nap. As much as possible, avoid eye contact with your baby when you're trying to put him to sleep. That would only encourage the baby to snap out of him sleep zone.

When you see any of these signs, quietly put your baby to bed.

How to teach your baby to sleep soundly

Babies do not yet know how sleeping works. As a parent, it is essential for you to teach your baby or toddler how and when to sleep. Following a routine is very helpful. As soon as your baby wakes up in the morning, open the curtains to allow sunlight to set into your home. This would let the baby know that it is time to wake up. Do this every morning until the baby gets used to it. You may want to have background music on, something lively like nursery rhymes. When you have bathed and fed him, play with your baby. You should only play with your baby during the day. At night, dim all lights and put some soothing music on. Prepare your baby for bed about two hours before bedtime. You may read him a book. Do not expose your baby to bright lights so he would know the difference between day and night. If the baby tries to cry after putting him down, just pat the baby gently. Tell him it's okay because you're around. You may lie down together and cuddle her. Try to pretend you're also asleep so he knows it's really time to go to bed. Avoid carrying your baby while putting him to sleep. He becomes dependent on it over time.

You could also try these other tips:

- Allow your baby to sleep on his own between six to eight months. This will make him not dependent on you all the time. When you see signs that the baby is already sleepy, gently put the baby to sleep. If she cries, pat her gently.

- Try massaging your baby before sleeping. Before doing this, make sure the room is pleasant and comfortable to set the right mood. The massage should last not more than 15 minutes.

- Give the baby a security object like a clean stuffed animal or a fresh baby blanket. For breastfeeding moms, try putting some breast milk on a piece of fabric and put it beside your baby. Since babies have strong sense of smell, the smell of the fabric may calm her.

- Always attend to your baby's needs. If she wakes up crying in the night, find out why. Check her diapers as it might be full. Or your baby could be hungry.

- Don't allow your baby to stay up too late. If he is still awake at 9pm, you might want to check his nap schedule. Schedule it in the early afternoon, not a couple of hours before bedtime.

- When you feed him during the night, stay quiet. Avoid chatting with your baby so he knows it's time for bed.

Sleep problems and solutions for babies:

Problem: Your baby is awake at night and asleep during the day.

This means the baby still isn't aware that nighttime is for sleeping. To help your baby sleep, take her outside during the day. Socialize and play with her. Be active. You could take a walk in the park with your baby. Inside the house, allow plenty of sunlight to get in. Play some active music. Watch less television. At sundown, dim the lights and turn off television. Music should be soothing. Avoid a lot of talk with the baby to encourage him to sleep.

Problem: The baby wakes up in the middle of the night.

Do not turn on the lights when your baby wakes up. This shift might tell her brain it's time to wake up. What you can do is carry the baby for a few minutes then put the baby back in the bed. Wait for a few minutes until he is settled in, then leave the room quietly.

Chapter 4: Gentle Ways to Put your Toddlers to Sleep

Toddlers need adequate sleep every night for their emotional and cognitive development. But they're very active and don't seem to want to go to sleep. When they're very tired and sleepy, they fight it. And they never get tired of playing. If you have a very challenging toddler, try these tips:

- Help him set his biological clock. Set a time for sleeping every night. If possible, let him prepare for bed early, say about 7 pm. Avoid letting him sleep late or when he's very tired. When a toddler is exhausted, his adrenalin and cortisol levels kick in. This would only keep him going. When this happens, toddlers find it harder to sleep during the night, and they wake up too soon. Dim the lights so he knows it's time to sleep. Avoid bright lights in his bedroom. Make him comfortable. His bed should be cozy. You may want to have a clean stuffed animal beside him to let him sleep right away.

- Prepare a bedtime light snack for your toddler. Some toddlers prefer to eat before sleeping. While reading him stories, let him have a healthy snack and try something without sugar.

- Get him sunlight and fresh air during the day. Let them play and socialize with other kids. Toddlers tend to sleep soundly during the night when they are active during the day. Just don't let them play a few hours before bedtime. It might just re-energize them. If you're good with humor, make your toddlers laugh. It's good for them.

- Acknowledge your toddler's courage if he tries to sleep on his own. Talk to your toddler about sleeping alone and give him prizes in the morning if he doesn't cry or looks for you in his bed. Practicing motivation is good for the toddler. You can give him perhaps a new toy when you go out or food in the morning. Something he really likes to eat.

- If a toddler is afraid to sleep in the dark, try telling him cheerful stories before bedtime. If he wakes up from a scary dream assure him it's gone now and that you're always there for him. Never tell him it's not real as dreams may seem very real to them. Just tell your toddler there is no need to worry.

Sleep problems and solutions for toddlers

Problem: Your toddler keeps getting in and out of bed.

If your toddler is already on his bed, but he keeps getting out, the reason is he doesn't want to go to sleep yet. You might want to try to do something creative with him. Try reading or listening to some relaxing music. You could also talk to him about a story you've read. If this doesn't work out, ask him what he needs. If he wants to get out of bed, let him. It's okay to sometimes make the child feels he is in control so long as you don't do it often.

Problem: Your child is already in bed for hours and he still can't sleep.

The one reason children can't sleep right away is because they have been playing or taking naps perhaps 1 or 2 hours before bedtime. Make sure naps are in the morning or early afternoon. Also, do not let your child play when it's almost bedtime.

Developing good sleeping practices with your baby or child

Sleeping is important to everyone's well-being and growth. For children, it makes them feel refreshed and alive during the day. They are unlikely to be irritable if they have a good night's sleep. Children remain alert and sharp when they are well rested. To help your child develop good sleeping habits, try these tips.

- Try to minimize bedtime rituals. You may not completely eliminate this, but being with your baby every time he is about to go to bed would make him dependent on you. You can still nurse or sing to him at bedtime but make sure you place him in his bed when he is still awake. It is better if he gets used to his mattress so in case he wakes up, he will not look for you.

- Don't let your baby fall asleep with his bottle. If he gets used to it, he will depend on it as well. He will not be able to sleep without the bottle. The extra calories may also interfere with his body rhythms and might wake him up when his hungry or milk might pool on the baby's ear and will cause an infection. To avoid these, make sure you won't let him accustomed to have his bottle before bedtime.

- Don't sleep with your baby beside you. Helping your baby sleep on his own would make him become independent. It would also reduce anxiety. If he's already used to it, try to eliminate it slowly until he gets used to sleeping alone.

- Help him overcome his fear of being separated from you. At six months, your baby might feel abandoned if you're not with him when he sleeps. To avoid this, try to spend time with your baby about 15 minutes before he goes to bed. When he's already in his crib, talk for about five minutes and gently touch him. Then leave the room quietly.

Dealing with sleep problems

Bed-wetting

This is normal for younger children. This becomes a problem when the child is more than five years old and he still wets his bed at least twice a week. The best thing to do is let your child know it is a normal condition and that it is a no big deal. You should also tell the other family members to not tease your child if he wet his bed. To help eliminate this problem, you need to monitor your toddler's fluid intake. You could also try waking him up after a few hours. If this doesn't help, try to talk to your pediatrician. He might be able to give you other options to help your child overcome this problem.

Sleep Deprivation

When your child isn't getting enough sleep, he will have trouble concentrating. He may perform poorly in school too.

There are things you can do to find out if your child isn't getting enough sleep.

- Observe if your child falls asleep when inside the car.
- He doesn't wake up early in the morning.
- You will notice that your child is overly sensitive and very irritable.
- He sleeps way early than his usual bedtime.

If you see these signs, try to adjust his routines for him to have quality sleep every night.

Chapter 5: Colic and How to remedy it

One of the challenges of being a parent is when a baby cries for hours for no reason. Colic is a condition where babies less than 4 months old cries for about 3 hours a day and 3 days a week. This happens to healthy babies, and it can be really stressful for a parent, but don't worry as it goes away after 3 or 4 months.

The cause of this condition is unknown. There were research done about colic, but they still couldn't figure out why it happens to healthy babies. Some of its symptoms include:

Crying episodes happen the same day every day for a few minutes to up to three hours. What a parent should do when this happens: Check your baby after crying as he might pass gas after a colic episode.

Intense crying. Colic is mysterious. No one really knows why it happens. When your baby cries, he is inconsolable. Nothing will make him stop crying.

Crying for no reason. When your baby has colic, he cries for no reason at all and you might notice some changes in the baby. He might clench his fists during a colic episode.

Some babies do not have Colic. Mothers who smoke before and after pregnancy contributes to an infant's colic.

Breastfed infants and first-borns are also not prone to colic. Colic disappears after 3 or 4 months. If it doesn't and you've tried doing everything to soothe your baby, talk to your pediatrician.

Here's what you can do before you make that appointment: Track how many times your baby cries and how many minutes or hours. Then write down how you've tried soothing your baby. You may list down other questions you have for the pediatrician.

Tips for soothing your baby:

- Hold your baby gently during a colic episode. Hold them upright to prevent them to swallow air.
- Have your baby burp after feeding.
- Bath and massage your baby. This is very helpful and may calm the baby.

Chapter 6: The Art of Napping

Establishing good napping habits for kids is just as important as establishing good sleeping habits. Napping, both for daytime and afternoon naps provide different benefits for babies and toddlers. REM sleep, which happens during daytime naps, is associated with brain development, while non-REM sleep, which happens during afternoon naps, is associated with psychological or emotional developments.

- Babies up to 18 months usually take a couple of naps in the morning and in the afternoon, while 18-month old babies up to three years, drops two naps to only one nap. This is okay so long as your child doesn't have any behavioral problems. Continue to monitor your child as he grows. If you notice that he is overtired, you may want to adjust his sleeping schedule.

- Consistency is the key when setting a nap schedule for your kids as it would help set their biological clock. The perfect time to nap is a few hours before bedtime so it wouldn't interrupt their sleep. Make sure the room is comfortable and pleasant enough to encourage sleep.

- Napping shouldn't be taken lightly by the parents as the child's emotional and cognitive growth also depends on it. Here are some benefits of napping:

- A child learns better if he naps. True, the child would easily remember information given to him if he naps within a 24-hour period compared to a child who doesn't nap at all. And it's not only his brains that can benefit from napping; it also impacts his physical growth.

- A child behaves well if he naps. When a child has adequate sleep, he performs better physically and emotionally. Kids who don't nap are usually very irritable.

- A child sleeps better at night. It is not true that when a child doesn't nap, he has longer sleep. In fact, he will find it hard to sleep if he doesn't nap. He is also more likely to have interrupted sleep.

Chapter 7: 4 Steps to Helping your Baby Sleep Soundly

Step 1: Create a Sleep Journal

Monitoring your child's sleeping pattern in the form of a sleep journal would be very helpful for you. It would let you track your child's progress or if there is a need to revise your sleep plan.

What to write in your Sleep Journal:

- Time your baby's sleep. Include naptime as well.

- You observations during your baby's sleep (if he is able to sleep with soothing music on, or not; if he wakes up during the night or early morning)

- Take note of the sleep strategies that work best for your baby.

- Review your journal every two weeks. If your strategies are working, continue doing it. Otherwise, change plans.

Step 2: Create a Sleep Plan

Sleep strategies help babies sleep soundly. However, it is also important to make sure that the baby's bedroom is safe, secure, comfortable, and quiet. Get a comfortable bed for your child or toddler. You might want to include some stuffed toys to play with. Make sure they are clean. Then review all the tips outlined in this book and see which ones work best for your child. Write them in your journal as well, so you can monitor the progress.

Step 3: Commit to your Plan for 10 Days

Try to be consistent with your baby's sleep schedule. One advantage is he will get used to sleeping in at same time every day. Consistency is always the key. If you fail, do not despair. Just keep trying and see which one works. Eventually, your hard work will pay off.

Step 4: Analyze your Child's Sleep Journal

After two weeks, check your journal for improvements, or if there is a need for you to change or revise your plan. If the plan works, continue doing it. If it doesn't, check the book again for more tips.

One thing to remember: Make sure your baby sleeps at least five hours each night. If your baby keeps waking up during the night, you might want to revise your sleep plan. Try other strategies that might work for your kid.

If you have not seen any progress, be patient. Carefully read the journal again. Perhaps you need to acknowledge a couple of small positive changes. Small things count. Just do it one day at a time. Remember, things take time. Just keep doing what works best, and change what needs to be altered.

There might also be a chance that things beyond your control are slowing your progress, like teething or other medical problems. When this happens, consult your pediatrician.

Safety precautions for families:

Never allow a smoker inside your child's bedroom. Babies exposed to second hand smoke face major health complications. If you have a family member who smokes, make sure he doesn't do so near your baby.

- Do not use thick comforters or blankets to cover your baby. It might entangle him.

- If your baby plays with stuffed toys, do not leave it on his bed. Once he's asleep, take them out.

- Pets are beautiful creatures, but don't give them access to your sleeping baby.

- Make sure your baby is near enough you can actually hear him when he cries or calls for you. Do not hang toys or things over your sleeping baby.

Chapter 8: Common Sleep Questions

This last chapter would be common sleep questions that parents want answers to:

How do I know if the baby is getting adequate sleep?

The only way to find out if your baby is getting enough sleep is to observe his overall behavior. A well-rested baby is normally happy and active. He also performs well in school and is mentally alert. However, a baby that's not getting enough rest at night will be grumpy and irritable. If your baby easily gets mad or annoyed, perhaps you would like to check his sleep habits. The Sleep Journal would be helpful.

Why is the baby fighting sleep?

One reason a kid fights sleep is because he doesn't want to miss out on anything. Kids love to explore. So if you are wide awake, they would want to be awake too. A tip: When it's about time for them to take a nap or to sleep, pretend you are also about to go to sleep with them.

How do you help your baby fall asleep at a different place?

There may be times when you will be going on vacation with your kids at some place far. Follow these tips to help your baby sleep soundly:

- Follow your sleep schedule. Wherever you are in the world, follow your child's regular sleep schedule.

- Bring baby things. If your baby sleeps with his stuffed toy, take it with you during the trip. You may want to also bring your baby's pillows or blankets. When he sleeps with those objects, the baby would think he's just at home.

- Let them sleep at Grandma's house. If you plan to go on vacation in a couple of months, arrange another trip at your parent's house. This is to pre-condition your baby to another environment. Still, you need to bring familiar objects with you so the baby is able to sleep right away. And, stick to the regular schedule.

- Take your iPod with you. Sometimes, a soothing or a calming music does the trick. When you're traveling with your baby, make it a point to always bring your mp3 or iPod with you. There is a power in a soothing music. It will surely help your baby sleep better.

Should I turn on or turn out the lights?

Use light-colored curtains if your baby is taking a nap. Do not expose the baby to bright sunlight. At least not that dark and not that bright either. You don't have to turn out all the lights at night. Your baby might cry if he doesn't see any light. Just dim the lights to induce sleepiness.

My baby keeps waking up in the middle of the night. Why is that?

There are several reasons why a baby suddenly wakes up several times a night. Check this list:

- The baby might be hungry. Infants, most especially, need to eat often for their growth. You may need to feed him in the middle of the night when you have to.

- A loud noise woke your baby up. To avoid this problem, you might want to sound-proof your baby's room. If you have other children in the house, you might want to ask them to keep the noise down to not wake the baby up.

- The baby is uncomfortable. Before you put the baby to sleep, make sure his clothes fit him well. Not too tight as that would surely wake the baby eventually. Check the baby's diaper as well. Perhaps it needs to be changed.

Is my baby sleeping too much?

You don't have to worry if your baby sleeps a lot. Babies do sleep a lot. They need it for their cognitive and physical growth. What you should worry about is when your baby is not sleeping enough.

Conclusion

Effective parenting creates an emotional bond between the child and parents. Infants, who are very attached to the mother, needs to be nurtured and cared for. They need to feel secure and protected. Before even planning to raise a family, it is important for both partners to plan ahead. Prepare for your pregnancy and how you will raise your child. After giving birth, make sure to breastfeed your child as that provides optimum health.

Touch is essential in building trust between the mother and the child. Give your baby or toddler lots of hugs, kisses, massage, or any physical contact that will soothe them. Co-sleeping with toddlers is also advisable; just don't do it every night.

However you want to raise your children, make sure you provide gentle and loving care.

Thank you again for downloading this book!

I hope this book was very helpful to you. Every child is different. Some tips may work for other children, and others won't. The next step is to try the tips found on this book and see which tips work best for your children.

Finally, if you enjoyed this book, then I'd like to ask you for a favor, would you be kind enough to leave a review for this book on Amazon? It'd be greatly appreciated!

Thank you and good luck!

Made in the USA
Columbia, SC
19 December 2022

74585532R00035